DOWNTON POSTCARDS

Mark O'Hanlon is a member of the Leintwardine History Society and has known Downton for thirty years. As an author and acknowledged local history expert, he recently contributed to the book, *Downton Gorge: The Matchless Valley*. Deltiology has been a developing interest and this new book brings to life his latest research.

DOWNTON POSTCARDS

Deltiology of the Downton Castle Estate, Herefordshire

MARK O'HANLON

First published 2022

ISBN 978-0-9528059-7-7

British Library Cataloguing in Publication Data. A catalogue record for this book is available from the British Library.

Printed in Great Britain by Craven Design and Print Ltd, Craven Arms

Published by
Mark O'Hanlon
5 Cangeford Drive
Ludlow
SY8 1XL

www.downtonpostcards.co.uk

Acknowledgements

Thanks to Tom and Gisèle Wall, and also to Viv Simkins (Archivist for the Leintwardine History Society), and to everyone who has contributed to my research or provided help and encouragement in locating images of the more scarce postcards of Downton, as credited within the Endnotes and Picture Sources section.

Special thanks to Steven Handy for taking on the typesetting and design work, and to William Troughton (Curator and Digital Archivist at The National Library of Wales) for presenting my findings on the P. B. Abery Collection to the library's Digitisation Committee, and for their subsequent updates to the library website.

Please note

Downton Gorge, Downton Castle and its environs are privately owned. The Castle is not open to the public, and there is no right of way through the Gorge.

Contents

Hay Mill,
near Ludlow.

Introduction

Postcards were available in the UK from 1870, but it is 1902-1918 that is regarded as 'The Golden Age of the Postcard'.[1] Fuelled by a change in postal regulations that from 1902 allowed the address and message fields to share a single side of the card, freeing up the other for a full-sided picture, card collecting became a popular pastime that was accessible to everyone. This was in addition to the benefits of sending short messages quickly and economically, for just half an old penny (½d).[2]

Downton Castle is located in Herefordshire, where the popularity of postcards peaked between 1905 and 1908,[3] so it is no surprise that it was during this period that Downton became the subject of many postcards. The Shropshire printers, L. Wilding of Shrewsbury (The Salop Art Press), were the most prolific.

With the rise in popularity, businesses were keen to sell postcards of their own. The larger printing companies either employed or commissioned photographers (of which there was a growing number) to produce images for their postcards. Smaller firms also entered the market – some producing their own

Opposite:
Figure I
Hay Mill, near Ludlow. Although the Downton Estate is located in Herefordshire, this postcard references Ludlow, just over the border in Shropshire, as it is the nearest town.

7

cards and others licensing from the larger firms. For example, Wilding allowed local stationers and newsagents with a large turnover of cards, to personalise stock cards with their own title and address.[4] However, many printers produced cards without any publishing attribution. As such, it can be difficult to catalogue postcards from this era.

One of the leading Victorian pioneers of the postcard phenomenon was Francis Frith (1822-1898). In 1860 he ambitiously set out to photograph every city, town and village in Britain.[5] Frith's studio was soon supplying retail shops all over the country. To meet the demand, he gathered about him a small team of photographers, and published the work of independent artist-photographers such as Francis Bedford (1816-1894) who we will discover more about later, in relation to Downton.

The Francis Frith Collection has been digitalised and contains a unique photographic archive of over 7,000

settlements across Britain.[6] Strangely, the archive contains no images of Downton Castle, despite Francis Bedford having photographed here. However, the success and influence of Frith's undertaking was a key driver in stimulating the growth in popularity of the postcard generally; and so Downton still featured on postcards by other publishers.

Downton Castle and the 'picturesque' landscape of the Downton Estate, was the brainchild of Richard Payne Knight (1750-1824). Having inherited a large fortune from his grandfather, the ironmaster Richard Knight (1659-1765), in 1772, the year after he came of age,[7] he set about designing and building his own house within the grounds of what was, at the time, one of the most productive ironworks in the country.

The building is a real curiosity; an enigma. Externally, it was built with gothic features resembling a castle. However, it was never designed for the practical purpose of fortification. Internally, it was given a Classical theme, with marble statues, pillars and pilasters and a circular dining room (with a domed roof) based upon the interior of the Roman Pantheon, located within the largest tower.

Richard Payne Knight was very vocal in promoting his love of the 'picturesque landscape' and so the 'Downton Walks' created within the castle grounds (which he presented as being a perfect example of this type of landscape) quickly became familiar to Knight's many learned friends and acquaintances.

The walks were open to the general public from the 1880s,[8] in the later years of Andrew Rouse Boughton Knight's (1826-1909) ownership, and continued throughout the stewardship of his son, Charles Andrew Rouse Boughton Knight (1859-1947), until at least 1949.[9]

Very little has been written on the topic of Downton deltiology (that's postcard collecting to the uninitiated!). This new book primarily focuses on the postcards produced in the early part of the twentieth century when the 'Downton Walks' became a cultural attraction (see Appendix).

Today, Downton Castle and the Downton Estate are privately owned and there is no public access; the exception being occasional guided walks through Downton Gorge organised by Natural England, who since 1982 have maintained a National Nature Reserve here. As such, the Downton postcards remain an important legacy, enabling us to view a part of the Herefordshire countryside that is otherwise not accessible to us today.

CHAPTER 1
Downton in the Pre-Postcard Era

O ne of the earliest examples of Downton being pictured on a card was a *Carte de Visite* or CdV showing the Castle's entrance towers across a fledgling fore-garden (Figure 1.1). Pre-dating the postcard era by decades, the CdV was a small photograph mounted on card (measuring just 2½" x 4") designed to be the size of a visiting card. Patented in Paris by photographer André Adolphe Eugène Disdéri (1819-

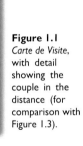

Figure 1.1
Carte de Visite, with detail showing the couple in the distance (for comparison with Figure 1.3).

11

1889) in 1854, these photographic cards were traded among friends and visitors in the 1860s.[10] Albums for their collection and display were common in Victorian times but unlike modern postcards, they were not designed to carry postal messages.

Clearly part of a much larger series, the Downton card is numbered and entitled: '468. Ludlow – Downton Castle, General View'. The publisher is unattributed and the card is difficult to date accurately but the image is almost identical to a photo contained in a personal album compiled by Thomas Andrew Knight's (1759-1838) daughter, Frances Stackhouse Acton (1794-1881),[11] so pre-dates 1881. The original photo has been cropped on all sides to fit the CdV format but that aside, the images are identical except for one small detail: the CdV card includes two people in conversation in the middle distance – a lady standing and a man seated on the garden wall.

Following extensive research, the Acton image can be attributed to Francis Bedford (1816-1894), a prominent landscape photographer who was active during the period 1852-1884; he received several royal commissions.[12] From the composition, it is very probable that both photos were taken at the same time and by the same photographer.

In his book *Ludlow Sketches* (1867), Thomas Wright (1810-1877) dedicates a whole chapter to Downton and includes a sketch of Downton Castle (Figure 1.3) that is remarkably similar to the CdV

Figure 1.2
Detail from a portrait of Francis Bedford (1815-1894). Bedford initially worked as a draughtsman before developing skills as a lithographer. In 1853 he took up photography and was elected to the London Photographic Society (now the Royal Photographic Society), becoming a Council member in 1857. Four years later he was elected Vice President.

photo – complete with a man and woman posing by the garden wall in the middle distance. Given that these images can be attributed to the same time period, this may not be a coincidence and could indicate the photo dates from the period 1852-1867. The artist has not been credited but is likely to have been Joseph Swain (1820-1909).[13]

Figure 1.3
Downton Castle, from *Ludlow Sketches* (1867), with detail.

Incidentally, Thomas Wright was born near Ludlow, at Tenbury Wells. He was educated at Ludlow Grammar School and at Trinity College, Cambridge. He was a founder member of the British Archaeological Association and the Camden, Percy and Shakespeare Societies. In 1842 he was elected corresponding member of the Académie des Inscriptions et Belles-Lettres of Paris, and was a fellow of the Society of Antiquaries, in addition to being a member of many other British and overseas learned societies.[14] As such, he would have moved in the same academic circles as the Knight family, and in his book demonstrates a detailed knowledge of their family history, the intricacies of Downton Castle and the layout of its picturesque landscape (see Appendix).

It is possible Thomas Wright knew Downton from a young age. His father, also named Thomas Wright,[15] provided valuable insight on Downton in *The History and Antiquities of the Town of Ludlow, and its Ancient Castle* which included a chapter dedicated to 'Gentlemen's Seats in the neighbourhood of Ludlow'. Published in 1826, when his son was sixteen years old, he describes how: 'The walks at Downton, which are well known, and much visited by travellers, extend to the west, following the course of the river which here occupies a deep ravine'.

Downton Castle was a private residence, so it is plausible that the couple shown in the photo and illustrated in the sketch are the castle owners. After all, although it was common practice for the wealthy to visit each other's estates, it seems unlikely that anyone other than the owners would pose in this way for such a formal photo by a renowned photographer that was then published as a CdV card. Further research might lead towards a conclusion that the couple shown are Andrew Johnes Rouse Boughton Knight and his wife Eliza, and it is easy to speculate as to the occasion.

Andrew Rouse Boughton Knight inherited Downton Castle in 1856, following the death of his father, Sir William Rouse Boughton of Downton Hall, Shropshire. At the time, Downton Castle having been rented out since 1852,[16] was tenanted by Joseph Jarrett but he and his family vacated the castle, moving to Ludford House near Ludlow in 1858. This enabled Andrew Rouse Boughton Knight to take up residence and to continue building work started by his father. A significant part of this work had already involved the construction of an additional tower and private chapel; completed in 1852.[17] The final stage of this particular scheme of work was internal to the castle, where the three downstairs bedrooms were converted into a sociable ballroom space, the bathrooms improved and the servants' quarters increased;[18] quite a significant alteration and modernisation of the original building of the 1770s, designed by Richard Payne Knight. In this context it would be conceivable that upon taking up occupancy, Andrew Rouse Boughton Knight would be keen to showcase the upgraded castle which is just what he did, in addition to celebrating his inheritance.

In December 1858, the Boughton Knights threw a spectacular Ball, opening their refurbished home to five hundred guests.[19] This would have been the perfect opportunity for Andrew and Eliza Rouse Boughton Knight to pose for a formal photograph against the backdrop of the castle's new façade and freshly laid gardens (as seen in Francis Bedford's photograph and in the CdV image, and in the sketch for Thomas Wright's book); if not in December 1858, then perhaps into the following year as part of an extended celebration.

The scheduling of the ball was reported in the *Hereford Times* and so the timing is beyond doubt. However, the hypothesis surrounding the timing and occasion of Francis Bedford's photograph, while tantalisingly plausible, remains inconclusive pending further research. At the very least though, it narrows the window on the photograph's origin to the period 1858-1867; the very height of CdV popularity and fashion.

Downton Church

Downton Castle.

Bridge and Dell near Downton Castle

CHAPTER 2
The Salop Art Press

The Shropshire printers, L. Wilding of Shrewsbury (The Salop Art Press), were the most prolific producers of Downton postcards. In 1904 they printed five different scenes, focusing on the Castle and grounds (serial numbers 562-566).[20] This was followed in 1906 by a further six scenes (serial numbers 1082-1087), with these aligned more to the wider area, including the 'Downton Walks',[21] which was the main draw for day trippers and tourists.

Longworth Wilding (1850-1918) was founder of the family business. Having originally trained as a telegraphist working at Shrewsbury Railway Station, at the age of twenty-four he married Emily Susan Ellis. In the following year, 1875, he purchased a property at 33 Castle Street, Shrewsbury and established his own business as a stationer, bookseller and printer.[22]

The printing industry experienced significant growth in the late nineteenth century. In addition to their bread-and-

Opposite:
Figure 2.1
Downton Church.
Figure 2.2
Downton Castle.
Figure 2.3
Bridge and Dell, near Downton Castle.

butter work of printing paper bags, commerce forms, ledgers and account books, the Wildings' business expanded rapidly. They took on more interesting and intricate publications, amongst them the *Directory of Shrewsbury* in 1893, the *Directory of Shropshire* in 1903 and the first edition of a publicity guide, *Church Stretton Illustrated*, followed in 1906 by *Shrewsbury Illustrated*. Closely associated with the production of these guide books were Wildings' first venture into the printing of postcards which saw considerable growth from 1903.

Wildings' adoption of the 'Salop Art Press' branding is of some interest. Originally attributed in 1890 to the firm Fred W Jarvis, a Commercial and Fine Art Printer based at 1 St Julian's Friars, Shrewsbury this particular firm ceased trading in the 1890s. It is unclear whether the business was then taken over but certainly Wilding used the trading name extensively from 1893 to 1910.[23] The motif conjoined the Salop Art Press and L. Wilding names, and the logo was used prolifically on the Wilding postcards from 1904 (Figure 2.4). This coincided with publication of the first Downton postcards.

Figure 2.4
The combined Wilding and Salop Art Press motif appeared on their early Downton postcards, with later postcards featuring just 'Wilding & Son'.

Many of the Wilding postcards are characterised by having a white border around the photo image. This was not uniform, and often had a wider margin on the right where they sometimes printed the card reference number (this has been cropped from the images reproduced here, in order to present a more aesthetic image for a twenty-first century audience).

The initial group of five postcards was published in

1904. Postcard 562 (Figure 2.1) shows, from across the field, the exterior of 'Downton Church' (the Church of St. Giles) that had been built within the castle grounds by Andrew Rouse Boughton Knight, and consecrated in 1862. The architect and contractor was Samuel Pountney Smith of Shrewsbury, who was responsible for building and restoring a large number of churches and other prominent buildings during the period 1840-1883.[24]

Simply entitled 'Downton Castle', postcard 563 (Figure 2.2) shows the castle from the south, across the Castle Meadow, above the River Teme. Prior to alterations made to the building by Sir William Rouse Boughton which were completed in 1852, this would have been the first view of the castle that visitors would have seen on their approach; the original castle entrance

Figure 2.5
Downton Castle.

19

Downton Lodge.

Figure 2.6
Downton Lodge.

having been on the southern façade.

Postcard 564 (Figure 2.3) entitled 'Bridge and Dell, near Downton Castle' shows the path to Stonebrook Cottage,[25] Richard Payne Knight's hideaway located a short walk from the castle. The gothic structure of the bridge is arguably over-engineered but carries what at the time of the photo had become the main driveway, over the dell, to the 'new' entrance on the northern façade of the castle building.

Postcard 565 (Figure 2.5) is the most popular of the castle images, if its ready availability to postcard collectors over one hundred years later is anything to go by! Simply entitled 'Downton Castle', it shows the castle entrance from the driveway on the north side which remains the main approach to the building today.

Postcard 566 (Figure 2.6) shows 'Downton Lodge'

which is the castle's main entrance gatehouse. The country lane disappears in the direction of Downton-on-the-Rock, and the assorted farms and cottages of the Downton Estate.

In 1906, a further six postcards were released by Wilding, showing additional scenes at Downton.

Figure 2.7
Downton Church interior.

Postcard 1082 (Figure 2.7) entitled 'Downton', presents something of an anomaly. The postcard shows the interior of Downton Church but two examples of this card have come to light: one in black and white (matching the rest of the series), the other printed with a colour tint. This appears to be contemporary with the card, and coloured so neatly as to rule out any after-market tampering.

'Downton Vicarage' is the subject of postcard 1083 (Figure 2.8). Like so

many parishes of the day, the vicarage (built later than the church, in 1883) has impressively rambling proportions and is located just along the lane from Downton Church.

Figure 2.8
Downton Vicarage.

Postcard 1084 (Figure 2.9) entitled 'Downton Castle' shows a close-up of the castle across the southern and western aspects, from the south terrace. It is an angle

that was also adopted by other publishers of the day, and makes an interesting comparison to other similar views, in terms of garden layout and maintenance (note the wall creeper has been trimmed significantly since the postcard images of 1904).

Postcard 1085 (Figure 2.10) is a portrait image of 'The Hay Mill – Downton' and takes the photographer into the picturesque landscape of the castle's 'Downton Walks'. The old mill was one of the most photographed features of Downton Gorge, and is the subject of several postcards by other publishers.

Continuing the 'Downton Walks' theme, 'The Bow Bridge at Downton' features on postcard 1086 (Figure 2.11) and is the postcard

22

scene furthest upstream from the castle, within the Wildings' series. The bridge marks the extremity of the Downton Walks, and its unusual design incorporates a single stone arch topped by a wooden parapet.

Finally, the Wilding series is completed at Downton with postcard 1087 whose catalogue entry is simply entitled 'At Downton' (Figure 2.12). This postcard is particularly interesting as it shows a 'pony bridge' (note the bridge is anchored on each river bank but there are no mid-stream supports) spanning the River Teme adjacent to the Hay Mill. What is unusual though, is that the postcard serial number indicates it was first published in 1906 and yet by then this particular construction had been replaced (pre-1905) by a new bridge which was supported mid-stream by two substantial supports (see Chapter 4).

Wilding had a very relaxed approach to printing the rear of each card. Whilst a mid-green coloured font

Figure 2.11
The Bow Bridge at Downton.

Opposite:
Figure 2.9
Downton Castle
and **Figure 2.10**
The Hay Mill –
Downton.

23

always predominated, other colours were periodically introduced. These included red, black, grey, brown and blue. There was no science behind the choice – it was simply influenced by whichever colour happened to have been loaded into the printing machine from the previous job.[26]

Figure 2.12
At Downton.

The Wilding business continued to trade through successive generations of the family until 1968 when the company was acquired by Stanley Sheridan Holdings. Over the next ten years, the company was asset-stripped and generally suffered from a subsequent loss of reputation. In January 1973, the retailing interests of Wildings were acquired by the Midland Educational Company, a Birmingham-based school supplier partnership with a general interest in books, stationery, artist materials and toys. The Wilding printing works were finally closed in 1982.[27]

CHAPTER 3
Heyworth and the Abery Anomaly

An intriguing set of Downton postcards often attributed to Percy Benzie Abery (1876-1948), a prominent Welsh photographer based in Builth Wells, are more likely to be the work of Robert Newton Heyworth (1877-1935), a photographer based in Knighton. The attribution to Abery comes from the images having been among a set of over one thousand five hundred glass negatives that Abery donated to The National Library of Wales, prior to his death in 1948.

Figure 3.1
West End Studios, Builth Wells.

Fifty years prior to this, in 1898, Abery bought a small photography business in Builth Wells. By 1911 his business had outgrown the premises and he moved to the West End Studios, nearby (Figure 3.1). The new studios were much bigger, with darkrooms in the basement, retail shop premises on the ground floor, a workshop for framing and mounting above, and finally a studio on the top floor (strategically located to take best advantage of daylight for his studio sittings).

During the summer months, Abery was often out and about on his bicycle (with camera and tripod on his back). A core part of his business involved photographing tourists as they 'took the waters' in both Builth Wells and nearby Llandrindod Wells. The following morning, groups would gather outside his shop window, looking for pictures of themselves to purchase. In due course, the bicycle gave way to a motorcycle, resplendent with side car, and then in 1928 his first car, which was an Austin.

Figure 3.2 Downton Rocks, with detail showing Heyworth's distinctive lettering.

Another aspect of his business was photographing weddings and local newsworthy events. Abery was also appointed official photographer by Birmingham Corporation Water Works, documenting the building of the Elan Valley Reservoirs, from where an aqueduct

DOWNTON ROCKS. (JKCT)

26

still carries water across Downton Gorge *en route* to Birmingham.

The Downton cards in question include a hand-written caption, along with lettering that appears to read 'CT. IK' – reversed to 'IK CT' on the 'Downton Rocks' image (Figure 3.2), showing the old quarry (which is adjacent to the Bow Bridge, towards the southern end of the gorge).

Rather than Abery, an alternative proposition, suggested by local deltiologist David Evans in his book *Border Wanderings: Photographic Studies by Robert Newton Heyworth of Knighton* (2008), attributes the postcard monogram to Heyworth, and that 'IK' is actually a conjoined 'HK'. Upon reflection, this is a strong argument, for although he doesn't suggest it directly, 'HK' could then refer to 'Heyworth Knighton' and 'CT' possibly to 'Copyright' (although the latter was not a recognised abbreviation); terms that by way of apparent confirmation, Heyworth has been found to have written in full on some photo images of other locations. For example, a postcard of nearby 'Wigmore Castle' dated 1919 is annotated '(Copyright) HK'.

Percy Benzie Abery was already well established in Builth Wells when, in 1905, Robert Newton Heyworth, who was at this time, it seems, working as a photographer, married in his home town of Rochdale. The following year the newly-weds relocated to the peace and tranquillity of the Welsh border country. Heyworth is believed to have taken over the photography studio of Edwin Debenham, and initially set up shop in West Street, Knighton.

Heyworth's relocation to Knighton was perfectly

timed to capitalise on the growing popularity of the postcard phenomena, and judging from his prolific output of photos and postcards over the following years, his new business flourished, and he quickly became a respected photographer in

Figure 3.3
Broad Street, Knighton, with detail.

his own right.

As the business grew, he relocated to larger, more central premises at 21 Broad Street, from where he soon expanded further, also taking neighbouring premises at 24 Broad Street. Reproduced in Figure 3.3 is one of Heyworth's own postcards of Knighton, looking down Broad Street from the Clock Tower. The shop with the bay window just down the hill on the left-hand-side is number 21, shown here with a young lady looking into the shop. Just off camera at the top of the hill on the same side of the street, is the much larger premises of 24 Broad Street.

There are a number of highly recognisable traits that

28

accompanied Heyworth's postcard images: his distinctive handwriting (he mainly wrote in capitals and often emphasised key letters by dropping them below the line) and the use of handwritten annotation to describe postcard scenes; the decorative detail or 'squiggle' that often underlined his annotation; the noting of image reference numbers (normally numbers followed by a letter), and finally, the marking of his initials as a monogram (Heyworth inter-changed between annotating 'CT. IK', 'IK CT' and 'IK', where 'IK' is actually a conjoined 'HK'). It was rare for all the traits to appear together but, more commonly, one or two are to be found on each of his postcard images.

David Evans didn't specifically review the Downton

Figure 3.4
Downton Castle Entrance.

postcards in either of his published books, but it is notable that 'Downton Castle Entrance' (Figure 3.4) showing the castle from the main driveway approach, featured Heyworth's decorative squiggle adjacent to the caption. This styling, along with a hand-written title, also featured on 'Downton Castle' (showing the castle from the south terrace), although this particular image has no monogram (Figure 3.5). Evans shared examples of other local postcards (including nearby Leintwardine) following similar design traits, all acknowledged as being the work of Robert Newton Heyworth.

Another photograph, 'Downton Church' (Figure 3.6), also carries the 'CT HK' monogram and can be attributed to Heyworth. Although to date no postcard

Figure 3.5
Downton Castle
and **Figure 3.6**
Downton
Church.

30

has come to light, given that it was amongst the glass negatives donated by Abery we should perhaps assume that, like the other Downton images amongst the set, this one was also reproduced as a postcard. As will be explained in the next chapter, all four of the Heyworth photos are believed to date from around 1906, making them some of the earliest ones he took following his relocation to Knighton.

Abery also annotated his cards but whereas Heyworth preferred capital letters, on the whole the output from Abery's studio was more varied; possibly suggesting he also had staff annotating them. For example, his annotations often used script, with joined up lettering. A good example of this can be seen on a postcard entitled 'Lion Hotel Leintwardine' (the building was sold from the Downton Estate, on 29 May 1919) that carries his studio acknowledgement on the rear (Figure 3.7). There are also many similar examples amongst his postcards of the Elan Valley reservoirs.

Figure 3.7
Lion Hotel, Leintwardine.

Overleaf:
Figure 3.8
Downton map.

31

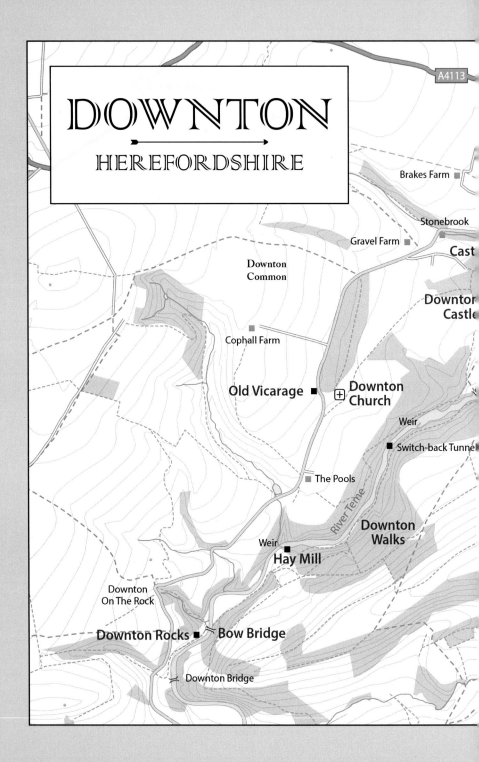

DOWNTON
HEREFORDSHIRE

A4113

Brakes Farm ■

Stonebrook

Gravel Farm ■

Cast

Downton
Common

Downtor
Castle

Cophall Farm ■

Old Vicarage ■ ⊞ Downton
Church

Weir

Switch-back Tunne ■

The Pools ■

River Teme

Downton
Walks

Weir
Hay Mill ■

Downton
On The Rock

Downton Rocks ■ Bow Bridge

Downton Bridge

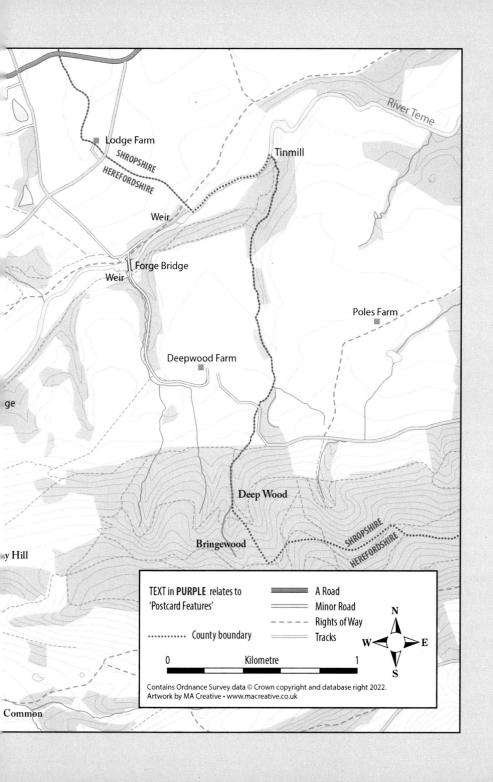

River Teme

Lodge Farm

SHROPSHIRE
HEREFORDSHIRE

Tinmill

Weir

Forge Bridge

Weir

Poles Farm

ge

Deepwood Farm

Deep Wood

y Hill

Bringewood

SHROPSHIRE
HEREFORDSHIRE

TEXT in **PURPLE** relates to
'Postcard Features'

·········· County boundary

━━━ A Road

━━━ Minor Road

- - - Rights of Way

━━━ Tracks

N
W ◆ E
S

0   Kilometre   1

Contains Ordnance Survey data © Crown copyright and database right 2022.
Artwork by MA Creative • www.macreative.co.uk

Common

Equally there are other Elan examples utilising capital lettering: one style, very neat and precise with the first letter of each word enlarged; another, much less precise but with lettering broadly uniform in size, rather than raised or lowered.

Both photographers produced postcards of Leintwardine and the Welsh border countryside. However, widening the research area has uncovered examples of postcards that carry both the 'CT. IK' monogram in combination with Heyworth's own studio stamp on the rear; further evidence that the monogram belonged to Heyworth rather than to Abery.

There are still some anomalies. Identical multi-view postcards of Leintwardine exist, with and without Heyworth's monogram; as does a postcard of Sarah Fairbank's Post Office in Church Street (Figure 4.9). Even more significantly, a postcard of Hightree House in Leintwardine displays Heyworth's handwriting and decorative squiggle but carries a clear statement on the rear indicating: 'Photograph by P. B. Abery, West End Studios, Builth Wells.' How could there have been this publishing mix up?

There is a suggestion by David Evans in his book *Border Wanderings*, that when Heyworth (who died in 1935) realised his health was failing, he may have allowed Abery to take over his business.[28] Evans admits he has found no evidence to fully substantiate this, but it would explain the anomalies pointed out above. Most importantly it would also explain how some of Heyworth's negatives came to be among those donated by Abery to the National Library of Wales,[29] leading to their erroneous attribution.[30]

CHAPTER 4

The Other Downton Postcards

O ther card producers also printed scenes of
Downton. Locally, cards were commissioned
by R.E. Crundell & Son (the 'Caxton Press') and
J. C. Austen, both of Ludlow, and by Sarah Fairbank at
nearby Leintwardine.

EYRE AND SPOTTISWOODE

Eyre and Spottiswoode were a printing company of
enviable pedigree, having served as both
the King's Printers and the Queen's
Printers (serving His / Her Majesty's
Stationery Office, respectively) under
more than one British monarch. Charles
Eyre received the company's first patent
as the King's Printer in 1767 but more
patents followed over the years, as successive
generations of the family continued to trade in
collaboration, as Eyre and Spottiswoode.[31]

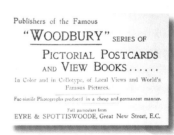

Figure 4.1
Placed in 1904,
advertisement for
the Woodbury
range of
postcards.

In 1878, the company diversified into the production
of Christmas cards. With the invention and growing
popularity of the postcard, it was then a natural

transition for them to become a key publisher in this burgeoning field through the introduction of their extensive 'Woodbury Series' of postcards.[32]

Postcard number 2689 within the Woodbury Series entitled 'Hay Mill, Near Ludlow' was a colour-tint photograph of the Hay Mill at Downton (Figure 1). An identical image reproduced in black and white, was also published as 'Downton. Hay Mill' (Figure 4.2). This card was published without accreditation and so may have been produced under licence by a different printer but is known to pre-date 1919.[33]

The original image of the Hay Mill scene was cropped on the left-hand-side in order to fit the rectangular postcard format. In his book, *Downton Gorge, Richard Payne Knight's Secret Garden* (2016), Barney Rolfe-Smith reproduces the full image from the original lantern slide, crediting it as having come from a collection of slides sold at an Edinburgh auction in 2016. He explains the photo is believed to have been taken in the late 1880s by a Dr John Ellis.

Figure 4.2 Downton. Hay Mill. The anonymous, monochrome, version of the same image as the colour Eyre & Spottiswoode card used on page 6 of this book (Figure I).

The mill is shown in a comparatively poor state of repair but, noting the rising smoke from the chimney beyond, it would appear the adjoining house was still occupied. Rolfe-Smith suggests two structures can be made out within the darkness of the tree line – one probably being the bridge, the other possibly a wooden structure known as the *moss house* (which would have had a bench and an open side facing the cliffs), used as a shelter for visitors. This helps to date the scene, although these particular features are not visible in the postcard images.

Eyre and Spottiswoode became part of Associated Book Publishers in 1958, merging with Methuen in the 1970s to become Eyre Methuen, and from 1987 were absorbed further through a series of subsequent company mergers and acquisitions.[34]

CRUNDELL

R. E. Crundell & Son were stationers operating from premises at the Bull Ring in Ludlow where they also traded as the Caxton Press; a photographic printing firm. Both trading names adorned their shop front (Figure 4.4). Their postcard of Downton also acknowledges both trading names but we find printed discretely on the back of other assorted local postcards of the period, 'R. C. Crundell & Son, Stationers, Ludlow' without crediting the Caxton Press.

Figure 4.3 Crundell motif, and **Figure 4.4** their premises in the Bull Ring, Ludlow.

Their Downton postcard is serial number B63406 and was entitled 'The Hay Mill, Downton, Nr Ludlow.' It shows a wide-angle view of the mill, and downstream panorama along the scenic banks of the River Teme (Figure 4.5). Of particular note are the two redundant stone piers standing mid-stream. Over the years there were a number of bridges constructed at this location but none survived for long and so the image is difficult to date. However, up to at least 1900 a 'Pony Bridge' spanned the Teme without any mid-stream support (Figure 2.12) but perhaps this was not deemed to be safe, as by 1905 piers had been added (Figure 4.14).

Figure 4.5
The Hay Mill, Downton, Nr Ludlow.

A bridge designed with supports would presumably have been more robust, and yet the absence of a bridge structure in the postcard would indicate it could not have had much longevity, as anecdotal evidence from contemporary postmarks indicate the photo is pre-1918.[35] Like the Eyre and Spottiswoode photograph of the mill, the original Caxton Press image has been cropped (this time at the bottom) to fit the postcard dimensions.[36]

AUSTEN

J. C. Austen were printers in their own right, in addition to being stationers. Operating from premises at 58 Broad Street in Ludlow (Figure 4.6), they produced a wide-ranging selection of local postcards, including colour and black and white images of Downton.

'Downton Castle' is an image of the castle looking north-east across the south terrace (Figure 4.7), and is very similar in aspect to Wilding 1084 (Figure 2.9) and to Robert Newton Heyworth's postcard of the same name (Figure 3.5). However, we know from the serial number that the Wilding postcard was first published in 1906, and judging by the extent of creeper on the castle walls, the Heyworth photo appears to date from

Figure 4.6
The Austen premises in Broad Street, Ludlow.
Figure 4.7
Downton Castle.

the same period. The Austen photo on the other hand, predates them both by a couple of years, as indicated by the more extensive growth of creeper on the left-hand and central towers, which match those of Wilding 563 (Figure 2.2) which was first published in 1904. Clearly the creeper was pruned over the intervening period. There were two versions of this card: one in colour and the other in black and white.

'The Hay Mill, Downton' is a close-up of the old mill from the banks of the River Teme (Figure 4.8). Although this card was printed portrait rather than landscape, both cards carry the accreditation 'Austen Ludlow' in the bottom right-hand corner. It is likely they both date from around 1904, which would place 'The Hay Mill, Downton' earlier than Wilding 1085 (Figure 2.10) of the same name, itself proven to date from 1906.

Figure 4.8
The Hay Mill,
Downton.

FAIRBANK

Situated just a few miles from Downton is the village of Leintwardine where for many years Sarah Fairbank, née Overton, (1854-1938) was the sub-postmistress. She held the position for over 60 years, having first been appointed around the age of twenty-one. She married the local vet, David Fairbank, in 1897; he was ten years her junior.

Census records show that by 1911, the Fairbanks were occupying a modern red brick house in Church Street (Figure 4.9)[37] opposite Leintwardine's St Mary Magdalen Church.[38] The house was called 'Fernleigh' and appears to have been purpose-built for them.[39] The door on the left gave access to the Post Office shop, while the door on the right opened into the veterinary surgery (observe 'Surgery' in the frosted window glass). Their living accommodation was above.

Sarah Fairbank started printing postcards around 1904 and is understood to have produced around forty designs over the next thirty or so years. She died in 1938, after which her husband was registered as being both postmaster and vet. He died just a few years later, in 1942.[40]

Amongst the many postcards of the Leintwardine area commissioned by Sarah Fairbank, three related to nearby Downton. Two of the postcards were both named 'Downton Castle' and were printed in the same style, with a band at the bottom of the card carrying the name and accreditation to Fairbank, in red lettering. One shows the castle from the north-east, looking south-west across the terrace (Figure 4.11). The other shows the south-west side of the castle across the formal gardens and period water feature (Figure 4.12). When considering the castle creeper, along with anecdotal evidence from contemporary postmarks, both cards date from around 1904 and so would presumably have been amongst her earliest designs.

The third postcard is in a very different style and is captioned 'Downton Castle Walks' (Figure 4.14). It shows the old Hay Mill and the downstream river banks upon which the pathways of the 'Downton Walks' were linked via a 'Pony Bridge'. Noting the earlier observations of a similar scene, this postcard image shows the later bridge fully intact. Postmark evidence dates the image as pre-1905.

Figure 4.9
Robert Newton Heyworth's postcard of the Post Office in Leintwardine.

Figure 4.10
Sarah Fairbank (1854-1938).

Figure 4.11
Downton Castle.

MYSTERY POSTCARDS

Two as yet unattributed postcard images have tantalisingly come to light, with very little detail. The first postcard is dated 1906 and shows two people stood upon the Bow Bridge (Figure 4.15). It is particularly unusual as the bridge is normally shown as a landscape view but this postcard is portrait. This creates a more dramatic image, by highlighting the steep-sided

Published by S. Fairbank, Leintwardine.   Downton Castle.

Figure 4.12
Downton Castle.

Figure 4.13
Leintwardine postmark.

Figure 4.14
Downton Castle Walks.

N CASTLE WALKS

Figure 4.15
Bow Bridge.

Figure 4.16
Downton Castle.

geography of the gorge to best effect in relation to the river.

The second postcard, like so many of the others, is simply entitled 'Downton Castle' (Figure 4.16). The castle has been photographed from a similar angle to Wilding 1084, taking in the southern and western aspects of the building from across the south terrace, but from further back across the lawn. This particular example is postmarked 1925, but the photo is likely to be earlier.

The creeper on the tower and castle walls is much thicker than in the earlier photos but other than that, provides no real indication as to age. By far the best evidence would appear to be the shrub on the left of the picture. It has large proportions and the positioning is not an obvious match to the garden layout of the early 1900s. Although taken from a different angle, later photos of the castle and gardens (as published by *Country Life* magazine in 1917),[41] prove the existence of the large shrub in the late 1910s. The wall creeper is less tamed and a little lower in relation to the first floor windows. This indicates the photo may in fact date from around 1918; potentially making it one of the last Downton Castle postcards of the period.

For completeness, local author Barney Rolfe-Smith has kindly shared an additional photo of Downton Castle purporting to be a postcard image (Figure 4.17).

This dates from 1954 which is curious, as it sits outside the main window of the 'Downton Walks' and features a very distant view of the castle. The presentation of the image has a home-made look and feel, which includes the lengthy but very precise caption: 'Panoramic view taken from Bringewood, on grass slope above road and ferns, across River Teme at Castle Bridge.'

In 1954 Downton Castle was owned by Major William Mandeville Peareth Kincaid Lennox. He was passionate about bulbs, especially daffodils. Many different varieties were planted in the castle grounds and he and his wife would open the gardens to the public each spring for annual Daffodil Days, with the proceeds going to charity.[42]

Whilst he is remembered for having a relaxed approach to locals accessing the private grounds of Downton Gorge, the area was not officially open to the public. As such, whilst the castle would still have been of interest, it would not have been an obvious choice for featuring on a postcard during this period. It is worthy of note that this particular angle, although less striking due to distance, perfectly captures the approach view originally intended by Richard Payne Knight when he built the castle in the 1770s with the castle featured resting at ease within its naturally picturesque landscape.

Figure 4.17
Downton Castle, Herefordshire 1954.

.DOWNTON CASTLE-HEREFORDSHIRE.
1954

Panoramic view taken from Bringewood, on grass slope above road and ferns across River Teme at Castle Bridge.

45

Postscript

This book has primarily focused on postcards published in the first half of the twentieth century. When the 'Downton Walks' closed to the general public around 1949, there was no reason to continue capturing Downton on postcard images. As such, we must fast-forward thirty years to complete this study.

In 1982, the Whitworth Art Gallery hosted an exhibition on 'The Arrogant Connoisseur: Richard Payne Knight (1751-1824)', in collaboration with Manchester University. A book of the same name, edited by Michael Clarke and Nicholas Penny, was published to accompany the exhibition. The cover illustration reproduced a portrait of Richard Payne Knight by Sir Thomas Lawrence (1769-1830) and this image was also printed as a postcard by the Friends of the Whitworth[43] (Figure 5.1). Although not specifically of Downton, it is included here for completeness, as Downton featured prominently in the exhibition and accompanying book, effectively having been put on the map by this postcard's subject, Richard Payne Knight.

In 1994, an exhibition was organised by a group of

academics (this time in collaboration with Hereford Art Gallery and Nottingham University Art Gallery), to celebrate the bicentenary of two seminal books on the aesthetics of landscape: Uvedale Price's *Essay on the Picturesque* and Richard Payne Knight's didactic poem, *The Landscape*.

Thomas Hearne (1744-1817) was commissioned by Richard Payne Knight to paint twelve watercolour scenes of Downton Gorge (1784-1786), to enable him to more easily share the experience of his picturesque landscape with family and friends. In 1994, two of these paintings were reproduced as postcards, in support of 'The Picturesque Landscape' exhibition.[44]

'The View Upstream' (Figure 5.3) captures the view looking upstream from the Switch-back Tunnel which is a feature of the 'Downton Walks'. This image was also used to illustrate the cover of a book which was published to accompany the exhibition.[45]

Figure 5.1 Richard Payne Knight, portrait by Sir Thomas Lawrence (1769-1830).

'The Cliff opposite the Hay Mill' (Figure 5.4) was painted from the north bank of the River Teme looking downstream towards the Hay Mill. Here the river is slowed by a weir, channelling the water to the mill wheel on the opposite bank. Contemporary plans (1780) indicate there was once a bridge behind where Hearne would have been sitting to paint this scene. Review the image carefully, and you may spot the artist has painted a woman walking along the pathway towards him.[46] In addition to being reproduced as a postcard, this illustration was also used as a frontispiece in the exhibition book.

It is rather fitting that Hearne's colourful scenes of Downton Gorge, which were originally commissioned by Richard Payne Knight to promote his picturesque landscape, should bring to a close our study of the postcards that promoted Downton throughout the postcard era of the twentieth century.

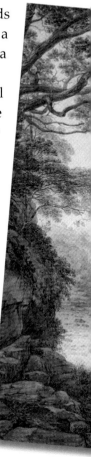

Researching the history of Downton postcards has proved to be an enjoyable challenge and one can only hope that time will be kind in proving this study to have been comprehensive. However, as postcard production in the late nineteenth and early twentieth centuries was rather ad hoc, and entry to the market was open to everyone, there is always the possibility that some cards have inadvertently been missed.

With this prospect comes the excitement that more postcards, as yet 'undiscovered' by this study, may come to light in the future, bringing with them fresh interest for those who are fortunate enough to make the discoveries.

Figure 5.2 'Portrait Study of Thomas Hearne', by William Daniell (1769-1837). Thomas Hearne (1744-1817) was born at Brinkworth, near Malmsbury. He trained as an engraver and later became a watercolourist. From 1781 to 1802 he exhibited at the Royal Academy.

In the meantime, hopefully cataloguing the thirty Downton postcards contained within this volume will help to stimulate the general conversation about Downton Castle and its picturesque landscape. That invigoration, more than anything, is bound to bring to life more material and expand our knowledge of this admittedly niche area of Herefordshire countryside, along with its associated deltiology.

Figure 5.3 'The View Upstream' and **Figure 5.4** 'The Cliff opposite the Hay Mill', both by Thomas Hearne.

The 'Downton Walks'

The existence and cultural attraction of Richard Payne Knight's 'Downton Walks', maintained by successive generations of the Knight family, was the main reason that Downton was on the map in terms of postcard production at the beginning of the twentieth century. At the time, the Rouse Boughton Knights allowed public access to the walks along Downton Gorge, and so it was only natural that visitors would want to purchase postcards so as to share their experiences with family and friends.

The 'Downton Walks' were a series of paths laid out in close proximity to the banks of the River Teme at Downton, where a number of natural and faux features partly created by limestone rocks channelling the river through a steep-sided gorge, had been incorporated within the riverside setting. Knight had used natural features to add interest, drama and romanticism to the visitor experience, presided over by his impressively bespoke house that had been designed to sit naturally within its adjoining landscape.

The most personal description outlining the principles of the 'Downton Walks' can be found within

Opposite:
Figure 6.1
Scenery like this attracted visitors to the 'Downton Walks'. This is a digitally enhanced version of Thomas Hearne's 'The View Upstream' (see pages 48-49 for comparison). We have used segments, again enhanced, from Hearne's 'The Cliff opposite the Hay Mill' on some of the following pages.

Richard Payne Knight's own treatise on the subject. First published in 1794, *The Landscape, a didactic poem in three books* ran to 1,300 lines, and was arguably his most enduring written work. Illustrated by three engraved plates by B. T. Pouncy, it served to show an imaginary house and landscape before and after 'improvement'; encapsulating Knight's preference for the former, which he argued was 'naturally picturesque' rather than man-made. This fuelled part of the 'Picturesque Controversy' that was then running, between exponents such as Uvedale Price (1747-1829) who shared Knight's view of the 'picturesque', and proponents of what they both regarded as being the more artificial landscaping styles, of Lancelot 'Capability' Brown (1716-1783) and Humphry Repton (1752–1818).

Over the years, much has been written about Richard Payne Knight, Downton Castle, his picturesque landscape and his 'Downton Walks'. However, to pick out three quotations that are particularly relevant to our study of Downton postcards, we should first return to the work of Thomas Wright.

In 1826, Thomas Wright (father of the celebrated antiquary of the same name, discussed in Chapter 1), shared an insight on the 'Downton Walks' within his book, *The History and Antiquities of the Town of Ludlow and its Ancient Castle*.[47]

The walks of Downton, which are well known, and much visited by travellers, extend to the west, following the course of the river which here occupies a deep ravine, that it appears to have worn during the lapse of ages. Upon the sides of this ravine the rocks have in places, where the texture has been firm, remained perpendicular over the stream; in other parts they have given way and fallen into the course of the river, and been carried away by its impetuosity. The ground consequently rises from each side of the river in very various and irregular forms; and it is every where clothed with timber; and the river, having a considerable descent and being confined within a narrow course, ripples over a succession of low falls. Much picturesque scenery is consequently presented, which varies as it is beheld from every successive point.

The walks, which have been made at different elevations along the sides of the ravine, have been conducted with much taste and art, though these will scarcely be seen by the careless observer; for the natural character of the place has been as much preserved as possible, and the direction of the walks appears at first view to have been regulated by a regard to convenience only.

In 1867, Thomas Wright (his son), dedicated a whole chapter to Downton in his own book *Ludlow Sketches*.[48] It gave a potted history of the Knight family, described the internal and external architecture of the castle, and of course explored in detail the 'Downton Walks'.

Downton Castle stands on the summit of a bank which rises to an elevation of about a hundred feet above the bed of the river. If, instead of entering the private grounds which surround the house, we take a lane which runs immediately under them, it will lead us down to a bridge... Above the bridge, the valley

changes into a narrow ravine, or chasm, formed by some primeval convulsion of nature, and the river runs down rapidly over a rocky bottom, pent in on each side by heights which sometimes present themselves in the form of vast masses of perpendicular rock. We pass over the bridge, and immediately on the other side a small wicket leads into the walk originally laid out under the direction of Richard Payne Knight, which runs at a little elevation along the side of the steep hill which here forms the bank of the river, and

Figure 6.2
'The Hay Mill' by Joseph Swain (1820-1909), from Thomas Wright's 1867 book, *Ludlow Sketches.*

which is clothed above and below with thick copse.

At a short distance from the entrance, the path passes through a cavern of some magnitude, under an overhanging mass of rock, on emerging from which the scenery of the river bursts upon us in all its picturesque beauty. As the path winds round the side of the hill, this scenery presents a continual change, the river at one time rushing with violence through a narrow channel between precipitous rocks, at another settling into a dark and quiet pool, surrounded by

woods which rise from it in varying outlines. Seats are placed at some of the most beautiful points of view, on which the visitor may rest and enjoy them. At a distance of somewhat more than half-a-mile from the cave, we come to an open moss-house, furnished with seats inside, and situated in a remarkably beautiful position. Before us, looking up the river, stands a mill, known as the Hay Mill, at which, when our sketch was taken, the river was crossed by a picturesque alpine bridge, but which, alas! has now disappeared, carried away a few years ago by a flood. This object added so much to the beauty of the scene that it is sincerely to be hoped that ere long it will be restored…

After we pass the mill, the road turns off from the river, to return to it again a little higher up, at a spot where it is crossed by a bridge of one arch, called the Bow bridge. A lane runs hence up the hill to the village of Downton, usually called Downton-on-the-Rock. As we advance

from the Bow bridge, a little higher up the stream, a long extent of lofty perpendicular rock faces the river; but it has now been considerably broken into by the process of quarrying. From the village we may walk back across the park to Downton Castle.

Many, however, will prefer returning from the Hay Mill by the same path which led them to it, for it presents in the way back almost a new series of changes of scenery. Or, when the Alpine bridge was standing, they might have crossed over to the other side of the river, and at a short distance from it, two paths branch off, one leading up the hill to the castle, the other running down the bank of the river to the foot of the bridge by which we first crossed it.

Oliver Baker (1856–1939) was a Fellow of the Royal Society of Painter-Etchers (London) and a Member of the Royal Society of Artists (Birmingham). In 1889, just fifteen or so years prior to publication of the Downton postcards, he wrote *Ludlow Town and Neighbourhood*. It was a book that contained a series of sketches of its scenery, antiquities and geology, drawn and described in pen and ink, which included a wonderfully descriptive account of his visit to nearby Downton.[49]

Acknowledging once again that the 'Downton Walks' are located on private land to which today there is rarely the opportunity for public access, to accompany the visual postcard images we can gain a contemporary feel for the late-nineteenth and early-twentieth century landscape, from reproduction of Oliver Baker's account which we pick up upon his arrival at the hamlet of Downton-on-the-Rock (to the south of the gorge), where we left Thomas Wright.

Here we leave the carriage, which will go on by the road and wait on the other side of Downton Castle, while we go back down the lane to a point where there is a gate into the wood, and follow the cart-track, which descends steeply to a picturesque stone bridge with a wooden parapet. The water is deep and calm between rocky banks, of a peculiar green colour, and so clear that the trout can be seen disporting themselves in its transparent depths. Crossing the bridge, the path turns to the left along the river-side. On the opposite bank is a pretty cottage, half hidden in the rank vegetation, with its strip of garden-ground hardly distinguishable from the wooded bank which rises behind.

As we proceed, the open glade, through which the river sweeps with foaming current, soon narrows to

Figure 6.3
'The Teme at Downton' by Oliver Baker (1856-1939), from his book *Ludlow Town and Neighbourhood* (1889).

a wild and rock-bound cleft, where the trees, springing from crevice and fissure, wreathe themselves into fantastic sprays and masses, among which the sky is only seen at intervals. Fairly within the gorge the bank on this side recedes, and the trees are of large size, but on the opposite side the pale limestone rocks rise vertically from the water. Farther down there is a place where the timber has been felled, and there is an open space among the beeches, whose companions lie prone amid the flowers and brambles.

The river is still now, and glides beneath the boughs almost noiselessly; but through the leaves comes the distant murmur of a weir, as yet invisible – faint at first, but growing louder at each step, till a turn in the path shows an old building through the stems, and below it the roofs of a larger one nestling under the bank, and then, as we descend into the level sward between the woods and the river, the loud roar of the pent-up stream bursts upon the ear. Our first impulse is to make for the narrow foot-bridge which spans the stream close to the house, and, on gaining it, the scene which meets our eyes is one which, far or near, it would be difficult to match for wild, secluded beauty.

On the left the Hay Mill, in the deep shade of overhanging trees, its mossy wheel half hidden by the grass-grown masonry which divides it from the river-bed and the pent-house roof overhanging it. Above the weir the trees stretch their branches so far as to completely choke the chasm with foliage. On the opposite side the grey limestone stands up from the water in a perpendicular cliff, to which the hazel and bramble cling in ragged luxuriance. For a long distance the woods approach the stream, often hanging over it, and the path continuing generally beside its edge, but sometimes mounting a slight eminence, gives great variety, and affords occasional peeps of fine reaches of river.

In one place the rock closes in upon the water, so that a passage has had to be hewn through it, and the path winds for a time through a romantic cavern. Not far from here a rather good saw-mill is passed on the other side the stream, and soon after the Castle Bridge, a stone structure of three arches, from which a pretty road winds up to the Castle... Ascending the slope, we see the castle is a very stately but incongruous edifice, placed in a most charming situation, and commanding views of extreme and varied loveliness.

In a foot-note, Oliver Baker duly acknowledges that at the time of writing in 1889, the walk through Downton Woods was accessible to the public on Tuesdays and Fridays, by the kind permission of its then owner, Andrew Rouse Boughton Knight.

Figure 6.4
Interestingly, this 1927 notice implores visitors not to damage the ferns, several decades after the Victorian 'Fern Craze' (Pteridomania) had fizzled out.

These written descriptions by our three quoted authors are included here to support in prose, the picturesque beauty of the area. In this way, they help to lift through colourful description, the visual legacy of the many contemporary black and white postcards that even today continue to feed the imagination, bringing alive the picturesque beauty of Downton, its castle and its celebrated walks, hand in hand with the surviving deltiology.

Endnotes

1   Farr J 2009, 14
2   Farr J 2009, 15
3   Farr J 2009, 14
4   Walley D M 1997, 34
5   Nicolle D 2002, 8
6   Nicolle D 2002, 10-11
7   Inglis-Jones E 1968, 246
8   Rolfe-Smith B 2009, 26
9   Wall T & G (Editors) 2022
10   Science and Media Museum https://blog.scienceandmediamuseum.org.uk/an-introduction-tothe-carte-de-visite/
11   Ionides J and Howell P 2006, 26 (noting that the photo is incorrectly attributed to FSA – our subsequent research has sourced an identical print within another personal collection, and confirmed that the photo was actually by Francis Bedford (1816-1894).
12   National Gallery of Art (US): https://library.nga.gov/permalink/01NGA_INST/puoc5q/alma991736003804896
13   The book *Ludlow Sketches* comprises a number of collated articles by Thomas Wright; many that had previously been published in the highly respected *Once a Week* magazine. Three of the eight illustrations (including one of the Hay Mill at Downton) are signed by Joseph Swain, who is known to have illustrated *Once a Week*, along with numerous other publications. He was one of the most prolific wood-engravers of the nineteenth century. Swain, who also exhibited at the Royal Academy, did not always sign his work so it is possible the five unsigned images (including Downton Castle), may be his work, as the *Ludlow Sketches* book contains no other attribution. Mayger Hind A 1912
14   Chisholm H 1911, 847
15   Oxford University Press 1975, 1045
16   Rolfe-Smith B 2020, 276
17   Rolfe-Smith B 2020, 276
18   Rolfe-Smith B 2013, 61
19   Rolfe-Smith B 2013, 61
20   Walley D M 1997, xliii
21   Walley D M 1997, xliii
22   Walley D M 1997, 13

23   Walley D M 1997, 16
24   Geroge D 1988, 1
25   The house has subsequently been renamed, Stonebrook Lodge.
26   Walley D M 1997, 34
27   Walley D M 1997, 28
28   Evans ATD 2008, 17
29   The National Library of Wales: www.library.wales/collections/learn-more/photographs/p-b-abery-collection
30   Note: Following this discovery, my research was shared with the Digital Archivist at the National Library of Wales. He has kindly confirmed his agreement with the research findings and an acknowledgment has subsequently been added to the Percy Benzie Abery Collection webpage. Whilst acknowledging that the accreditation of each individual image should also be reviewed and updated, the library regret they have insufficient resources to undertake this task at the current time.
31   *Grace's Guide to British Industrial History* (www.gracesguide.co.uk/Eyre_and_Spottiswoode)
32   Coysh A W 1996
33   Post-marked card within a private collection.
34   Penguin Random House Archive (https://archive.penguinrandomhouse.co.uk/History%20of%20Methuen%20Publishing%20-%20Opac%20version.htm)
35   Rolfe-Smith B 2009, 27
36   Rolfe-Smith B 2016, 43
37   Private collection. This particular postcard was produced by Robert Newton Heyworth of Knighton and carries his 'CT. IK' monogram in the bottom right-hand corner; a variant of the postcard also exists without the monogram.
38   Information courtesy of Viv Simkins (Archivist), Leintwardine History Society.
39   Williams J 2006: *Leintwardine History Society Journal* 17
40   Information courtesy of Viv Simkins (Archivist), Leintwardine History Society.
41   Avray Tipping H 1917, 39: *Country Life* magazine (14/07/1917)
42   Jackson E and Edwards M (Editors) 2000, 77
43   This postcard was also available at 'The Picturesque Landscape' exhibition in 1994. The card is an unusual size, measuring 6" x 4 3/8", and has a white band below the portrait image.
44   These were two of four postcards printed in support of the exhibition, the other two (not relating to Downton) being a portrait of Uvedale Price by Sir Thomas Lawrence, and Charlotte Davenport's painting, 'Cottage, Red Tiles, At Claypits, May 2nd 1861'. The cards were printed in the modern postcard

format of 6" x 4". The Whitworth Art Gallery's postcard of Richard Payne Knight by Sir Thomas Lawrence, was also on sale at the exhibition. Information courtesy of Charles Watkins and Tom Wall.

45   Daniels S and Watkins C (Editors) 1994
46   Wall T & G (Editors) 2022, 225
47   Wright T 1826, 226
48   Wright T 1867, 111-113
49   Baker O 1889, 124-128

Picture Sources

1   Eyre and Spottiswoode: Hay Mill, Near Ludlow. Private Collection
2   Mark O'Hanlon: Downton Castle (photograph). Private Collection
3   Gauci: Richard Payne Knight. From Gregory T 1824, *The Shropshire Gazetteer*
1.1   Bedford: CdV Card. Private Collection
1.2   Unknown: Francis Bedford © Wellcome Library (No. 14933i)
1.3   Unknown: Downton Castle (sketch). From Wright T 1867, *Ludlow Sketches*
2.1   Wilding 562: Downton Church. Private Collection
2.2   Wilding 563: Downton Castle. Private Collection
2.3   Wilding 564: Bridge and Dell, near Downton Castle. Leintwardine History Society
2.4   Wilding Motif. Private Collection
2.5   Wilding 565: Downton Castle. Private Collection
2.6   Wilding 566: Downton Lodge. Private Collection
2.7   Wilding 1082: Downton (Church Interior). Private Collection: John Farr
2.8   Wilding 1083: Downton Vicarage. Shropshire Archive (Ref. PC/D/9/19)
2.9   Wilding 1084: Downton Castle. Shropshire Archive (Ref. PC/D/9/1)
2.10   Wilding 1085: The Hay Mill – Downton. Shropshire Archive (Ref. PC/D/9/16)
2.11   Wilding 1086: The Bow Bridge at Downton. Leintwardine History Society
2.12   Wilding 1087: At Downton. Shropshire Archive (Ref. PC/D/9/14)
3.1   Abery: West End Studios. The National Library of Wales
3.2   Heyworth: Downton Rocks. The National Library of Wales
3.3   Heyworth: Broad Street, Knighton. Private Collection
3.4   Heyworth: Downton Castle Entrance. The National Library of Wales

Bibliography

Where authors' names and dates of publication are emboldened, the publications in question include substantive Downton content.

Avray Tipping H 1917, *Country Life* magazine (14/07/1917): 'Country Homes Gardens Old & New: Downton Castle, Herefordshire'

Baker O 1889, *Ludlow Town and Neighbourhood*

Chisholm H 1911, *Encyclopædia Britannica* Vol. 28 (11th ed.): 'Wright, Thomas'

Coysh A W 1996, *The Dictionary of Picture Postcards in Britain 1894-1939*

Daniels S and Watkins C 1994, *The Picturesque Landscape: Visions of Georgian Herefordshire*

Evans ATD 2008, *Border Wanderings: Photographic Studies by Robert Newton Heyworth of Knighton*

Farr J 2009, *The Picture Postcard Heritage of Herefordshire Churches*

George, D 1988, *The Church of Saint Giles Downton: A Guide for Visitors*

Inglis-Jones E 1968, *The National Library of Wales Journal* Vol. XV. No. 3: 'The Knights of Downton Castle'

Ionides J and Howell P 2006, *The Old Houses of Shropshire in the 19th Century: The watercolour albums of Frances Stackhouse Acton*

Jackson E and Edwards M (Editors) 2000, *Downton 2000: The story of the community at Downton-on-the-Rock and Downton Castle Herefordshire*

Mayger Hind A 1912, *Dictionary of National Biography (Supplement)*

Nicolle D 2002, *Francis Frith's Photographic Memories: Around Ludlow*

Oxford University Press 1975, *The Compact Edition of the Dictionary of National Biography*

Rolfe-Smith B 2009, *Notes on Bringewood Forge and the Downton Walks*

Rolfe-Smith B 2013, *Colonel John Colvin 1794-1871*

Rolfe-Smith B 2016, *Downton Gorge, Richard Payne Knight's Secret Garden*

Rolfe-Smith B 2020, *The Knight Family of Downton Castle Volume 1 1698-1852*

Wall T & G (Editors) 2022, *Downton Gorge: The Matchless Valley*

Walley D M 1997, *Greeting From Shropshire: Wilding's of Shrewsbury and their Postcards*

Williams J 2006, *Leintwardine History Society Journal* 17: 'Leintwardine's Postal History'

Wright T 1826, *The History and Antiquities of the Town of Ludlow and its Ancient Castle*

Wright T 1867, *Ludlow Sketches*